Developers' Guide to GANs and TensorFlow:

A Comprehensive Toolkit for Creating, Training, and Deploying Advanced AI Models

.....

Matthew D.Passmore

1

Chapter 10: State-of-the-Art GAN Architectures (e.g., StyleGAN)
10.1 Deepfakes and High-Fidelity Image Generation
10.2 Ethical Considerations of Advanced GANs

Chapter 1
What are Generative Adversarial Networks (GANs)?

Generative Adversarial Networks (GANs) are a type of deep learning system that uses two neural networks competing against each other to produce increasingly realistic and original data. Imagine it as a game between a forger and a detective.

The Generator: This network acts like the forger, trying to create new data (like images, music, or text) that closely resembles the real data it's been trained on. It starts with random noise and refines it to produce something that appears genuine.

The Discriminator: This network acts like the detective, analyzing both the real data and the generated data to identify which is which. It gets better at spotting fakes as the generator improves its forgeries.

Here's the key:

Through this ongoing competition, both networks improve. The generator gets better at creating realistic data, and the discriminator gets better at spotting fakes. This adversarial training helps the generator learn the underlying patterns and complexities within the real data.

What can GANs be used for?

GANs have a wide range of applications because they can generate new data types that are indistinguishable from real data. Here are some examples:

Creating photorealistic images: GANs can be used to generate new images of faces, landscapes, or even entirely new objects.

Generating new music: By analyzing existing music styles, GANs can create original pieces that mimic that style.
Data augmentation: GANs can be used to create more training data for other machine learning tasks, especially when real data is scarce.
Image editing: GANs can be used to manipulate images in creative ways, like adding or removing objects or changing styles.

The power of GANs lies in their ability to learn complex patterns and use them to produce entirely new and original data. As GAN research continues to develop, we can expect even more exciting applications in the future.

1.1 Core Concepts of GANs

GANs are a fascinating concept in deep learning, and understanding their core principles is crucial to using them effectively. Here's a breakdown of the key ideas:

1. Adversarial Training:

This is the heart of GANs. It involves two neural networks, the Generator (G) and the Discriminator (D), in a constant competition.

The Generator, like a forger, tries to create new data (images, text, etc.) that is indistinguishable from real data. It starts with random noise and transforms it through its layers to generate realistic outputs.

The Discriminator, like a detective, acts as the adversary. It analyzes both the real data and the generated data, trying to differentiate between them. As the Generator improves its forgeries, the Discriminator needs to become better at spotting fakes.

2. Loss Function and Gradient Updates:

Both networks have their own loss functions. The Generator's loss is measured by how well it can fool the Discriminator. Ideally, the Discriminator should classify the generated data as real as often as possible.

During training, the Generator and Discriminator are updated iteratively. The Generator's weights are adjusted based on the feedback from the Discriminator's loss function, helping it improve its forgeries. Similarly, the Discriminator's weights are updated based on how well it can distinguish real from fake data.

3. Convergence and Equilibrium:

The training process aims to reach a state of equilibrium. Ideally, the Generator becomes so good at creating realistic data that the Discriminator can no longer reliably tell the difference. However, perfect equilibrium can be challenging to achieve, and training stability is an ongoing area of research.

4. Types of GAN Architectures:

There are many variations of GAN architectures, each with its strengths and weaknesses. Some popular examples include:
DCGAN (Deep Convolutional GAN): A widely used architecture specifically designed for generating images.
WGAN (Wasserstein GAN): Addresses some training instability issues faced by earlier GAN models.

5. Applications of GANs:

The ability of GANs to produce high-quality, realistic data has opened doors to a wide range of applications:

Image and video generation: Creating photorealistic images, editing existing ones, or generating entirely new content.
Text generation: Creating realistic and coherent text formats, like poems or code.

Data augmentation: Expanding existing datasets by generating synthetic data for training other machine learning models.

Drug discovery: Simulating molecular structures to aid in drug development.

Understanding these core concepts lays the foundation for delving deeper into GANs and exploring their potential for various applications.

1.2 Applications of GANs

GANs have revolutionized various fields by creating new possibilities through their ability to generate realistic and original data. Here's a glimpse into some of the exciting applications of GANs:

1. Image and Video Manipulation:

Image Generation: Creating entirely new, photorealistic images of faces, landscapes, or even objects that don't exist. This can be used for generating artistic content, creating textures for 3D graphics, or even populating virtual worlds.

Image Editing: GANs can manipulate existing images in creative ways. Imagine adding or removing objects, changing styles (e.g., turning a photo into a painting), or even colorizing black and white photos.

Video Prediction: GANs can be used to predict the next frame in a video sequence, enabling applications like video editing, animation, or even creating realistic special effects.

2. Content Creation and Design:

Generating New Music: By analyzing existing music genres, GANs can create original pieces that capture the style and essence of that genre. This opens doors for music generation, composing soundtracks, or even creating personalized music experiences.

Character Design: For animation, video games, or graphic design, GANs can be used to generate new and unique character designs, helping artists explore creative possibilities and come up with fresh ideas.

3. Data Augmentation and Enhancement:

Data Scarcity Solution: In some machine learning tasks, real data might be limited. GANs can generate synthetic data that closely resembles real data, effectively expanding datasets and improving the performance of machine learning models.

Image Inpainting: Imagine restoring damaged or incomplete images. GANs can analyze the surrounding areas and fill in the missing parts, creating a realistic and seamless reconstruction.

4. Beyond Visual Media:

Text Generation: GANs are capable of generating different forms of text formats, like poems, code, or even scripts. This has applications in creative writing, generating realistic dialogue for chatbots, or even code completion for programmers.

Drug Discovery: Simulating complex molecular structures is crucial in drug development. GANs can be used to generate new molecule candidates that might possess desired properties, accelerating the process of drug discovery.

These are just a few examples, and the potential applications of GANs continue to expand as research progresses. As GANs become more sophisticated, we can expect even more groundbreaking applications across various industries. However, it's important to acknowledge the ethical considerations surrounding the use of GANs, especially when dealing with deepfakes or synthetic media that can be used for malicious purposes.

Chapter 2

Why TensorFlow for GAN Development?

TensorFlow has emerged as a powerful and popular choice for developing Generative Adversarial Networks (GANs) due to its robust features and extensive functionalities. Here's a breakdown of the key advantages TensorFlow offers for GAN development:

1. Flexible Architecture and Customization:

TensorFlow provides a low-level, flexible architecture that allows you to construct custom neural network architectures for your specific GAN needs. This is crucial for experimenting with different GAN variations (e.g., DCGAN, WGAN) or even creating entirely new architectures.

2. Powerful Computational Tools:

TensorFlow offers seamless integration with various hardware platforms, including GPUs and TPUs, which are essential for accelerating the computationally intensive training process of GANs. This allows you to train your models faster and experiment with more complex architectures.

3. Vibrant Community and Resources:

TensorFlow boasts a large and active developer community. This translates to a wealth of resources available online, including tutorials, code examples, and discussions specifically focused on GAN development with TensorFlow. You can easily find solutions and get help when facing challenges.

4. Integration with Other Tools:

TensorFlow integrates seamlessly with other popular machine learning libraries like Keras, which provides a high-level API for building neural networks. This allows you to leverage the ease of use of Keras while still benefiting from the low-level control offered by TensorFlow for building complex GAN architectures.

5. Scalability and Deployment:

TensorFlow is designed for scalability, allowing you to train large and complex GAN models on massive datasets. Additionally, TensorFlow Serving provides tools for deploying your trained GAN models into production environments, enabling you to integrate them into real-world applications.

Here's a quick comparison highlighting some key advantages of TensorFlow for GAN development:

https://docs.google.com/spreadsheets/d/1Vzj1nv_8e6YHI_a-skYCQplS8J7XlHw8saZ2JwxxAg/edit?usp=drivesdk

Overall, TensorFlow provides a powerful and versatile toolkit for developing and deploying cutting-edge GAN applications. Its flexibility, computational muscle, and strong community support make it a compelling choice for researchers and developers working with GANs

2.1 Advantages of TensorFlow for GANs

The realm of Generative Adversarial Networks (GANs) thrives on pushing the boundaries of artificial intelligence. To navigate this complex landscape, developers need a powerful and versatile toolkit. TensorFlow steps up to the plate, offering a compelling set of advantages that make it a champion for GAN development.

Here's a closer look at why TensorFlow stands out:

Unleashing Architectural Creativity: Unlike some frameworks with a more rigid structure, TensorFlow offers a low-level, flexible architecture. This empowers you to craft custom neural network architectures tailored to your specific GAN needs. Whether you're experimenting with established variations like DCGAN or WGAN, or even pioneering entirely new architectures, TensorFlow grants you the freedom to bring your vision to life.

Computational Powerhouse: Training GANs is no easy feat; it demands significant computational resources. TensorFlow tackles this challenge head-on with seamless integration with various hardware platforms. GPUs and TPUs, the workhorses of deep learning, become readily available for your GAN training. This translates to faster training times, allowing you to iterate more quickly and explore more complex architectures.

A Thriving Community by Your Side: The journey of a GAN developer is not a solitary one. TensorFlow boasts a large and active developer community. This translates to a wealth of resources at your fingertips. Online forums, tutorials, and code examples specifically focused on GAN development with TensorFlow become your companions. When you encounter roadblocks, you'll find a supportive community ready to offer solutions and share their expertise.

The Power of Collaboration: TensorFlow doesn't exist in isolation. It integrates beautifully with other popular machine learning libraries like Keras. Keras provides a high-level API for building neural networks, making the initial steps of development more user-friendly. This lets you leverage the ease of use offered by Keras while still retaining the low-level control of TensorFlow for building intricate GAN architectures. It's the best of both worlds!

Scaling Up and Reaching the Real World: As your GANs evolve, TensorFlow scales up with them. It's designed to handle large and complex models, allowing you to train on massive datasets and achieve groundbreaking results. But the journey doesn't end there. TensorFlow Serving provides the tools you need to deploy your trained GAN models into production environments. This crucial step lets you integrate your GANs into real-world applications, where they can unleash their true potential.

In conclusion, TensorFlow empowers GAN developers with a unique blend of flexibility, computational muscle, and a supportive community. It's a framework that scales with your ambition, allowing you to craft innovative GAN architectures, train them efficiently, and ultimately deploy them to make a real-world impact. Whether you're a seasoned GAN developer or embarking on your first project, TensorFlow is a powerful ally to have by your side.

2.2   Setting   Up   Your   TensorFlow   Development Environment

Before diving into the fascinating world of Generative Adversarial Networks (GANs), you'll need to establish a development environment equipped with TensorFlow. Here's a roadmap to guide you through the process:

1. Prerequisites:

Python: GAN development primarily revolves around Python. Ensure you have a recent version of Python (preferably 3.7 or above) installed on your machine. You can verify this by opening a terminal or command prompt and typing python --version.

Virtual Environment (Recommended): Creating a virtual environment is highly recommended. It isolates your GAN project's dependencies from your system-wide Python installation, preventing conflicts with other projects. Tools like venv (built-in) or conda can be used for this purpose.

2. Install TensorFlow:

Once you have Python set up, it's time to install TensorFlow. There are several ways to achieve this:

Using pip: This is the most common method. Open your terminal or command prompt and run the following command:
Bash

```
pip install tensorflow
```
Use code with caution.

content_copy

Using conda: If you're using Anaconda or Miniconda, you can install TensorFlow through the conda package manager:

Bash

```
conda install tensorflow
```

Use code with caution.

content_copy

3. Verify Installation:

After installation, it's good practice to verify if TensorFlow is working correctly. Create a simple Python script (e.g., test_tensorflow.py) with the following code:

Python

```python
import tensorflow as tf

hello = tf.constant('Hello, TensorFlow!')
print(hello)
```

Use code with caution.

content_copy

Run this script using python test_tensorflow.py. If everything is set up correctly, you should see the message "Hello, TensorFlow!" printed in your console.

4. Additional Considerations (Optional):

GPU Support (if applicable): If you have a Nvidia GPU and want to leverage its power for faster training, you'll need to install additional libraries like CUDA and cuDNN. Refer to the official TensorFlow documentation for detailed instructions on GPU setup.

TensorFlow Serving (for deployment): If you plan to deploy your trained GAN model, you might consider installing TensorFlow Serving. This toolkit helps you serve your model in production environments.

By following these steps, you'll have a robust TensorFlow development environment ready to tackle the challenges of GAN development. Remember to consult the official TensorFlow documentation for the latest installation instructions and specific configuration details for your operating system and hardware setup.

Part 2: Building GANs with TensorFlow

Chapter 3
Deep Dive into GAN Architectures

Generative Adversarial Networks (GANs) have revolutionized the field of generative modeling by enabling the creation of incredibly realistic and original data. But at the heart of every GAN lies its architecture, the blueprint that defines how the Generator and Discriminator networks interact and learn. Let's delve deeper into this fascinating realm:

1. Core Building Blocks:

Convolutional Neural Networks (CNNs): For image-based GANs, Convolutional Neural Networks (CNNs) are the workhorses. CNNs are adept at capturing spatial relationships between pixels, making them ideal for processing and generating images. They are frequently used in both the Generator and Discriminator for image tasks.

Dense Layers (Fully Connected Layers): These layers connect every neuron in one layer to every neuron in the next, allowing for more complex information processing. They are often used in the initial or final stages of networks, especially when dealing with non-image data like text.

Activation Functions: These functions introduce non-linearity into the networks, enabling them to learn complex patterns. Common activation functions used in GANs include ReLU (Rectified Linear Unit) and Leaky ReLU.

2. Popular GAN Architectures:

Deep Convolutional GAN (DCGAN): A widely used and successful architecture specifically designed for generating images. It leverages CNNs extensively in both the Generator and Discriminator. The Generator typically uses transposed convolutional layers (up-sampling) to gradually increase the resolution of the generated image, while the Discriminator uses convolutional layers (down-sampling) to extract features for classification.

Wasserstein GAN (WGAN): This architecture addresses some of the training instability issues faced by earlier GAN models. It introduces a new loss function, the Wasserstein loss, that helps to improve training stability and convergence. The network architectures themselves can vary, but often incorporate convolutional layers similar to DCGAN.

3. Architectural Variations:

Beyond DCGAN and WGAN, there's a vast world of GAN architectures, each with its strengths and applications. Here are a few examples:

Conditional GANs (cGANs): These GANs incorporate additional input alongside the random noise, allowing the Generator to produce outputs conditioned on that input. For example, a cGAN could generate images of different dog breeds based on breed labels provided as input.

StyleGAN: This powerful architecture has achieved impressive results in generating high-fidelity images. It leverages progressive growing techniques and introduces concepts like style vectors to achieve a high level of detail and control over the generated images.

4. Choosing the Right Architecture:

The best GAN architecture for your project depends on several factors:

Type of Data: For images, DCGAN or WGAN are often good starting points. For text generation, architectures with recurrent neural networks (RNNs) might be more suitable.

Desired Output Quality: More complex architectures like StyleGAN can achieve higher fidelity but require more computational resources and training data.

Project Requirements: Consider factors like training time, hardware limitations, and the level of control you need over the generated data.

Remember, this is just a glimpse into the ever-evolving world of GAN architectures. As research progresses, new and innovative architectures are constantly emerging, pushing the boundaries of what's possible. By understanding these core concepts and exploring different architectures, you can empower yourself to create GANs that tackle a wide range of creative and challenging tasks.

3.1 Understanding Generator and Discriminator Networks

Generative Adversarial Networks (GANs) are like a fascinating game played by two neural networks: the Generator and the Discriminator. Each network plays a crucial role in the process of creating ever-more realistic and original data. Let's delve into their inner workings:

1. The Generator: The Creative Force

Imagine the Generator as a skilled artist. It takes a source of randomness, often in the form of a random noise vector, as its raw material. This noise vector acts like a spark of inspiration, containing a tiny seed of an idea.
Through its layers, the Generator transforms this noise vector. It uses convolutional layers (for images) or dense layers (for other data types) to progressively build upon the initial spark, adding details and structure.

The goal of the Generator is to create a final output, like an image or a piece of text, that is indistinguishable from real data. It strives to mimic the complex patterns and distributions found in the real data it has been trained on.

2. The Discriminator: The Skeptical Critic

The Discriminator acts as the discerning art critic. It receives both real data (from the training dataset) and the generated data from the Generator.

Its job is to analyze each piece of data and determine whether it's authentic (real data) or a forgery (generated data). The Discriminator uses its own neural network architecture to extract features and make this critical judgment.

As the Generator improves its forgeries, the Discriminator needs to become even better at spotting fakes. This ongoing competition pushes both networks to learn and adapt.

3. The Learning Dance: Loss Functions and Gradient Updates

Both the Generator and the Discriminator have their own loss functions. These functions measure how well each network is performing its task.

The Generator's loss is calculated based on how well it can fool the Discriminator. Ideally, the Discriminator should classify the generated data as real as often as possible.

During training, both networks are updated iteratively. The Generator's weights are adjusted based on the feedback from the Discriminator's loss function. This helps the Generator refine its forgeries and get better at mimicking real data.

Similarly, the Discriminator's weights are updated based on how well it can distinguish real from fake data. As the Generator improves, the Discriminator needs to adapt its own strategies for identifying fakes.

4. The Art of Balance: Achieving Equilibrium

The training process aims to reach a state of equilibrium. Ideally, the Generator becomes so good at creating realistic data that the Discriminator can no longer reliably tell the difference between real and fake. This state, however, can be challenging to achieve, and training stability is an ongoing area of research in GANs.

In essence, the Generator and Discriminator are locked in a continuous game of one-upmanship. This adversarial training process is the heart of what makes GANs so powerful. By constantly pushing each other to improve, both networks learn to capture the intricate details and patterns of real-world data, enabling the Generator to produce ever-more realistic and creative outputs.

3.2 Popular GAN Architectures (e.g., DCGAN, WGAN)

Generative Adversarial Networks (GANs) come in many forms, each with its strengths and weaknesses. Here's a closer look at two popular architectures, DCGAN (Deep Convolutional GAN) and WGAN (Wasserstein GAN), along with code snippets to illustrate their basic structure:

1. Deep Convolutional GAN (DCGAN):

Description: DCGAN is a widely used architecture specifically designed for generating images. It leverages convolutional layers (CNNs) in both the Generator and Discriminator for effective image processing.

Code Example (using TensorFlow):

```python
Python
# Import libraries
import tensorflow as tf
from tensorflow.keras import layers

# Define Leaky ReLU activation
def leaky_relu(x, alpha=0.2):
```

```python
    return tf.maximum(x, alpha * x)

# Generator architecture (using transposed convolutions)
def build_generator(noise_dim, channels):
  model = tf.keras.Sequential([
            layers.Dense(7 * 7 * 256, use_bias=False,
input_shape=(noise_dim,)),
    layers.Reshape((7, 7, 256)),
    layers.BatchNormalization(),
    layers.LeakyReLU(alpha=0.2),
    # Up-sampling layers with transposed convolutions
            layers.Conv2DTranspose(128, (3, 3), strides=2,
padding='same', use_bias=False),
    layers.BatchNormalization(),
    layers.LeakyReLU(alpha=0.2),
            layers.Conv2DTranspose(channels, (3, 3),
activation='tanh', padding='same', use_bias=False),
  ])
  return model

# Discriminator architecture (using regular convolutions)
def build_discriminator(channels):
  model = tf.keras.Sequential([
    layers.Conv2D(64, (3, 3), strides=2, padding='same',
input_shape=(32, 32, channels)),
```

```
    layers.LeakyReLU(alpha=0.2),
    layers.Conv2D(128, (3, 3), strides=2, padding='same'),
    layers.LeakyReLU(alpha=0.2),
    layers.Conv2D(256, (3, 3), strides=2, padding='same'),
    layers.LeakyReLU(alpha=0.2),
    layers.Flatten(),
    # Final layer for classification
    layers.Dense(1),
  ])
  return model
```
Use code with caution.

content_copy

Explanation:

The build_generator function defines the Generator architecture. It starts with a dense layer followed by reshaping and batch normalization. Then, it uses transposed convolutional layers (Conv2DTranspose) to gradually increase the spatial resolution of the image, from a noise vector to the desired output size (e.g., 32x32 pixels for images with 3 channels). Leaky ReLU is used as the activation function throughout.

The build_discriminator function defines the Discriminator architecture. It uses regular convolutional layers (Conv2D) with strides of 2 for down-sampling the image and extracting features. Finally, it uses a dense layer with one unit and a sigmoid activation for binary classification (real or fake).

2. Wasserstein GAN (WGAN):

Description: WGAN addresses some training instability issues faced by DCGAN. It introduces the Wasserstein loss function, which helps improve training convergence.

Code Example (using TensorFlow):

Note: Implementing WGAN can be more complex than DCGAN. Here's a simplified example focusing on the core architecture:

```python
Python
# Import libraries
import tensorflow as tf
from tensorflow.keras import layers

# Gradient penalty for WGAN (omitted for simplicity)
# ...
```

```python
# Generator architecture (similar to DCGAN)
def build_generator(noise_dim, channels):
  # ... (similar to DCGAN example)

# Discriminator architecture (similar to DCGAN)
def build_discriminator(channels):
  # ... (similar to DCGAN example)
```
Use code with caution.

content_copy

Explanation:

The code structure for the Generator and Discriminator remains similar to DCGAN.

The key difference lies in the loss function used during training. WGAN utilizes the Wasserstein loss function instead of the traditional binary cross-entropy loss used in DCGAN. Implementing the gradient penalty, another crucial aspect of WGAN training, is omitted here for simplicity.

Remember: These are simplified examples for illustrative purposes. Real-world GAN implementations often involve additional complexities and hyperparameter tuning. It's recommended to consult the official TensorFlow documentation

Chapter 4
Implementing a GAN in TensorFlow

The world of Generative Adversarial Networks (GANs) can seem complex, but with TensorFlow as your companion, you can take your first steps towards creating your own. Here's a breakdown of the process, guiding you through implementing a basic GAN architecture:

1. Project Setup:

Ensure you have TensorFlow installed (refer to previous explanations for installation instructions).
Familiarize yourself with the basic concepts of GANs, including the Generator and Discriminator networks (refer to previous explanations for a deeper understanding).
2. Choose a Simple Architecture:

For beginners, start with a well-documented and relatively simple architecture like DCGAN (Deep Convolutional GAN). This architecture is specifically designed for image generation and leverages convolutional neural networks (CNNs) for effective image processing.
3. Define the Building Blocks:

Import necessary libraries like TensorFlow (tf), Keras (keras from TensorFlow), and other utilities like NumPy (np). Define functions for key components:

Noise Generator: This function will create random noise vectors as input for the Generator. You can use tf.random.normal to generate random numbers from a normal distribution.

Data Loader: This function will load your training data (images in this case). You can use libraries like tensorflow.keras.preprocessing.image for image loading and preprocessing.

Build Generator: This function will define the neural network architecture of the Generator. Refer to the DCGAN code example provided earlier for guidance on using convolutional layers, transposed convolutions, and activation functions.

Build Discriminator: This function will define the neural network architecture of the Discriminator. Similar to the Generator, use convolutional layers for feature extraction and a final layer for classification (real or fake).

4. Loss Functions and Optimizers:

Define the loss functions for both the Generator and Discriminator.

Generator Loss: This can be the negative of the

Discriminator's output for the generated images (assuming you want the Discriminator to classify them as real).
Discriminator Loss: This can be the sum of the loss for real images (classified correctly) and the loss for generated images (classified incorrectly).

Choose optimizers for both networks. Common choices include Adam or RMSprop.

5. Training Loop:

Implement a training loop that performs the following steps in each iteration:
Generate a batch of noise vectors.
Use the noise vectors to generate a batch of fake images with the Generator.
Load a batch of real images from your training data.

Train the Discriminator:

Feed the Discriminator with real and fake images separately.

Update the Discriminator's weights based on the Discriminator's loss.

Train the Generator:

Feed the Generator with noise vectors.

Update the Generator's weights based on the Generator's loss (which aims to fool the Discriminator).

6. Monitor and Evaluate:

Implement mechanisms to monitor the training process. You can track metrics like the Generator's loss and the Discriminator's accuracy.

Periodically save checkpoints of your trained model to allow for resuming training or evaluating the generated images later.

Here are some additional resources to help you get started:

TensorFlow DCGAN Tutorial: https://www.tensorflow.org/tutorials/generative/dcgan

MNIST Generative Adversarial Network (GAN) with Keras and TensorFlow: https://pyimagesearch.com/category/generative-adversarial-networks-gans/

Remember: This is a foundational guide, and real-world GAN implementations often involve additional complexities like hyperparameter tuning, data augmentation, and more advanced architectures. However, with this roadmap and the power of TensorFlow, you're well on your way to building and exploring the exciting world of GANs!

4.2 Building the Generator and Discriminator Models

Generative Adversarial Networks (GANs) have become a powerful tool for generating realistic and creative data. TensorFlow provides a robust framework for building and training GANs. This guide delves into the practical implementation of the Generator and Discriminator models, using a well-documented architecture like DCGAN (Deep Convolutional GAN) for image generation.

Prerequisites:

Basic understanding of GANs (Generator and Discriminator concepts)

TensorFlow and Keras installed (refer to previous explanations for installation)
Familiarity with Python programming

1. Define the Project and Data

Choose a dataset of images you want the GAN to learn from. For this example, we'll assume you have a dataset of human faces.
Preprocess the images to a uniform size and format (e.g., resize to 32x32 pixels and normalize pixel values between 0 and 1).

2. Import Libraries and Functions

```python
Python
import tensorflow as tf
from tensorflow.keras import layers
from tensorflow.keras.datasets import mnist  # Assuming MNIST dataset for simplicity

# Additional utility functions (optional)
import matplotlib.pyplot as plt
import numpy as np
Use code with caution.
```

content_copy

3. Define Helper Functions

Noise Generator:

This function creates a random noise vector as input for the Generator.

Python
```python
def generate_noise(batch_size, noise_dim):
    """
    Generates a batch of random noise vectors.

    Args:
        batch_size: The number of noise vectors to generate.
        noise_dim: The dimension of the noise vector.

    Returns:
        A tensor of shape (batch_size, noise_dim).
    """
    noise = tf.random.normal(shape=(batch_size, noise_dim))
    return noise
```
Use code with caution.
content_copy

Data Loader:

This function loads and preprocesses a batch of images from the training dataset.

Python
```
(train_images, _), (_, _) = mnist.load_data()  # Assuming
MNIST for simplicity
train_images = train_images.reshape(-1, 28, 28,
1).astype('float32') / 255.0

def load_data(batch_size):
    """
    Loads and preprocesses a batch of images from the training
    dataset.

    Args:
        batch_size: The number of images to load.

    Returns:
        A tensor of shape (batch_size, image_height,
        image_width, channels).
    """
    dataset = tf.data.Dataset.from_tensor_slices(train_images)
    dataset = dataset.shuffle(buffer_size=60000)
```

```
dataset = dataset.batch(batch_size)
return dataset.prefetch(tf.data.AUTOTUNE)
```
Use code with caution.

content_copy

4. Building the Generator Model

The Generator takes a random noise vector as input and transforms it into a realistic image. Here's a DCGAN-inspired implementation using transposed convolutions:

Python
```python
def build_generator(noise_dim, channels):
    """

    Builds the Generator model architecture.

    Args:
        noise_dim: The dimension of the noise vector.
        channels: The number of channels in the output image
    (e.g., 3 for RGB).

    Returns:
        A Keras model representing the Generator.
    """
```

```python
model = tf.keras.Sequential([
        layers.Dense(7 * 7 * 256, use_bias=False,
input_shape=(noise_dim,)),
    layers.Reshape((7, 7, 256)),
    layers.BatchNormalization(),
    layers.LeakyReLU(alpha=0.2),
    # Up-sampling layers with transposed convolutions
        layers.Conv2DTranspose(128, (3, 3), strides=2,
padding='same', use_bias=False),
    layers.BatchNormalization(),
    layers.LeakyReLU(alpha=0.2),
        layers.Conv2DTranspose(channels, (3, 3),
activation='tanh', padding='same', use_bias=False),
])
 return model
```

Use code with caution.

content_copy

Explanation:

The model starts with a Dense layer that projects the noise vector into a higher-dimensional space.

Reshaping and BatchNormalization layers prepare the data for the convolutional layers.

Leaky ReLU is used as the activation function throughout the network, allowing for gradients to flow even for negative inputs.

The core of the Generator lies in the up-sampling layers achieved using transposed convolutions (also known as deconvolutions). These layers progressively increase the spatial resolution of the feature maps, allowing the network to gradually build a complete image from the initial noise vector. Here's a breakdown of the up-sampling layers in the provided code:

Conv2DTranspose(128, (3, 3), strides=2, padding='same', use_bias=False):
This layer takes the output from the previous layer (likely with a lower feature map resolution) and applies a transposed convolution with 128 filters of kernel size (3, 3).

The strides=2 parameter indicates an upsampling factor of 2 in both height and width dimensions. This effectively doubles the spatial resolution of the feature maps.
padding='same' ensures that the output has the same spatial dimensions as the input, achieved by adding padding pixels around the borders if necessary.

use_bias=False avoids adding a bias term to the convolution, as BatchNormalization is applied afterwards.

BatchNormalization():

This layer normalizes the activations of the previous layer, helping to stabilize the training process and improve gradient flow.

LeakyReLU(alpha=0.2):

The Leaky ReLU activation function introduces non-linearity into the network. Unlike ReLU, which sets negative inputs to zero, Leaky ReLU allows a small positive gradient for negative values (controlled by the alpha parameter here set to 0.2). This helps to prevent the "dying ReLU" problem where gradients vanish during backpropagation.

Discriminator Model

The Discriminator acts as the art critic, evaluating the authenticity of images generated by the Generator. It aims to distinguish between real images from the training dataset and the generated fakes. Here's a typical Discriminator architecture using regular convolutions for down-sampling:

Python
def build_discriminator(channels):

"""

Builds the Discriminator model architecture.

Args:
    channels: The number of channels in the input images (e.g., 3 for RGB).

Returns:
    A Keras model representing the Discriminator.
"""

```python
model = tf.keras.Sequential([
    layers.Conv2D(64, (3, 3), strides=2, padding='same',
input_shape=(32, 32, channels)),
    layers.LeakyReLU(alpha=0.2),
    layers.Conv2D(128, (3, 3), strides=2, padding='same'),
    layers.LeakyReLU(alpha=0.2),
    layers.Conv2D(256, (3, 3), strides=2, padding='same'),
    layers.LeakyReLU(alpha=0.2),
    layers.Flatten(),
    # Final layer for classification (real or fake)
    layers.Dense(1, activation='sigmoid')
])
return model
```
Use code with caution.

content_copy

Explanation:

The Discriminator starts with a Conv2D layer that applies 64 filters of kernel size (3, 3) to the input image.

The strides=2 parameter in the convolutional layers performs down-sampling, reducing the spatial resolution of the feature maps while capturing higher-level features.

Leaky ReLU is used as the activation function throughout the network, similar to the Generator.

After down-sampling with convolutional layers, the features are flattened into a one-dimensional vector before feeding them to a final Dense layer with one unit and a sigmoid activation.

The sigmoid activation function outputs a value between 0 and 1, representing the Discriminator's probability of the input image being real (closer to 1) or fake (closer to 0).

Remember:

This is a simplified example, and real-world GAN implementations might involve additional layers, weight initialization techniques, and hyperparameter tuning.

The specific number of filters, kernel sizes, and strides can be adjusted based on the complexity of the data and desired output image resolution.

By combining these Generator and Discriminator models, you can establish the foundation for your TensorFlow GAN. In the next steps, you'll define the loss functions, optimizers, and training loop to train your GAN and generate realistic images!

4.3 Training Loop and Loss Functions

Now that you have the Generator and Discriminator models built, it's time to set the stage for their adversarial training dance. Here's a breakdown of the crucial elements involved:

1. Loss Functions:

Generator Loss: The Generator aims to fool the Discriminator into classifying its generated images as real. A common approach is to use the negative of the Discriminator's output for the generated images during backpropagation. This encourages the Generator to produce images that the Discriminator has a high probability of classifying as real.

Discriminator Loss: The Discriminator strives to accurately distinguish between real and fake images. Its loss function can be formulated as the sum of two components:

Loss for Real Images: This measures how well the Discriminator classified real images as real (ideally, close to zero loss).
Loss for Fake Images: This measures how well the Discriminator classified generated images as fake (ideally, close to zero loss).

2. Optimizers:

Both the Generator and Discriminator need optimizers to update their weights based on the calculated loss values during training. Popular choices include Adam or RMSprop, which efficiently navigate the complex optimization landscape of GANs.

3. Training Loop:

This is the core of the training process, where the Generator and Discriminator are iteratively pitted against each other. Here's a typical structure of a training loop in TensorFlow:

```python
Python
# Hyperparameters (adjust as needed)
learning_rate = 0.0002
batch_size = 32
noise_dim = 100

# Define optimizers for Generator and Discriminator
generator_optimizer                          =
tf.keras.optimizers.Adam(learning_rate=learning_rate)
discriminator_optimizer                      =
tf.keras.optimizers.Adam(learning_rate=learning_rate)

# Training loop
@tf.function
def train_step(real_images, noise):
  # Generate fake images
  fake_images = generator(noise, training=True)

  # Train Discriminator (freeze Generator weights)
  with tf.GradientTape() as disc_tape:
    # Discriminator loss for real and fake images
```

```
                                   disc_real_loss          =
discriminator_loss(discriminator(real_images,
training=True))
                                   disc_fake_loss          =
discriminator_loss(discriminator(fake_images,
training=False))
  total_disc_loss = disc_real_loss + disc_fake_loss

# Update Discriminator weights
                      discriminator_gradients              =
disc_tape.gradient(total_disc_loss,
discriminator.trainable_variables)

discriminator_optimizer.apply_gradients(zip(discriminator
_gradients, discriminator.trainable_variables))

# Train Generator (freeze Discriminator weights)
with tf.GradientTape() as gen_tape:
  # Generator loss (wants Discriminator to classify fakes as
real)
    gen_loss = generator_loss(discriminator(fake_images,
training=False))

# Update Generator weights
```

```python
    generator_gradients = gen_tape.gradient(gen_loss,
generator.trainable_variables)

generator_optimizer.apply_gradients(zip(generator_gradien
ts, generator.trainable_variables))

  return disc_real_loss, disc_fake_loss, gen_loss

# Example training loop usage
for epoch in range(num_epochs):
  for real_images in load_data(batch_size):
    noise = generate_noise(batch_size, noise_dim)
            disc_real_loss, disc_fake_loss, gen_loss =
train_step(real_images, noise)
    # ... (optional: log metrics, generate and visualize images)
```

Use code with caution.

content_copy

Explanation:

This code defines a train_step function that takes real images and noise vectors as input.

Inside the training loop:

Fake images are generated using the Generator.

The Discriminator is trained first with its weights frozen:

It calculates the loss for both real and fake images.

The total Discriminator loss is calculated and used to update its weights through backpropagation.
The Generator is trained with its weights frozen:
It calculates the loss based on how well it fooled the Discriminator.

The Generator's weights are updated through backpropagation.
This adversarial process continues for multiple epochs, allowing both networks to iteratively improve their performance.

Key Points:

Remember to define appropriate loss functions (discriminator_loss and generator_loss) based on your specific implementation.
The @tf.function decorator can improve training efficiency by converting the training step into a TensorFlow graph.

Sources
info
github.com/HenriARM/gan-art
github.com/neel-dey/Atlas-GAN subject to license (MIT)
github.com/Ahaeflig/probaVSuperRes

Part 3: Training and Fine-tuning GANs

Chapter 5
Preparing Your Data for GAN Training

Before diving into the training process, it's crucial to prepare your data effectively for optimal GAN performance. Here are some key steps to consider:

1. Choose the Right Dataset:

The quality and relevance of your dataset significantly impact the outcome of your GAN. Select a dataset that aligns with the kind of images you want to generate.
For example, if you want to generate human faces, a dataset of diverse facial images from various angles and ethnicities would be ideal.
2. Preprocessing:

Resizing and Cropping: Ensure all images in your dataset have a uniform size. Resizing and cropping might be necessary to achieve this.

Normalization: Normalize pixel values within a specific range (commonly 0 to 1 or -1 to 1) for consistency and efficient training.

Data Augmentation (Optional): Consider techniques like random flipping, cropping, or color jittering to artificially increase the size and diversity of your dataset. This can help the GAN learn more robust features.

3. Data Loaders:

Implement a data loader function or utilize existing libraries like TensorFlow's tf.data API to efficiently load and batch your data during training.

This ensures smooth data flow and avoids memory bottlenecks while training the GAN.

Here's a code example illustrating data loading with basic preprocessing:

```Python
def     load_data(batch_size,     image_height=28,
image_width=28, channels=1):
    """
```

Loads and preprocesses a batch of images from the training dataset.

Args:

    batch_size: The number of images to load.

    image_height: The height of the images.

    image_width: The width of the images.

    channels: The number of channels in the images (e.g., 1 for grayscale, 3 for RGB).

Returns:

      A tensor of shape (batch_size, image_height, image_width, channels).
    """

```
# Assuming you have your dataset loaded (replace with your data loading logic)
# ...

# Preprocess images
    images = tf.image.resize(images, (image_height, image_width))
images = images / 255.0  # Normalize pixel values between 0 and 1

dataset = tf.data.Dataset.from_tensor_slices(images)
dataset = dataset.shuffle(buffer_size=60000)
dataset = dataset.batch(batch_size)
```

```
return dataset.prefetch(tf.data.AUTOTUNE)
```
Use code with caution.

content_copy

Additional Considerations:

Data Cleaning: Address any potential issues in your data like corrupted images or missing values before training.

Class Imbalance (if applicable): If your dataset has imbalanced classes (e.g., fewer images of a specific type), consider techniques like oversampling or undersampling to balance the representation.

By meticulously preparing your data, you lay a solid foundation for your GAN to learn the underlying structure and generate realistic images. Remember, "garbage in, garbage out" applies to GAN training as well. Spend time ensuring high-quality and well-preprocessed data for optimal results.

5.1 Data Preprocessing Techniques for GANs

Data preprocessing is an essential step in preparing your dataset for successful GAN training. Just like a chef needs quality ingredients for a delicious dish, a GAN requires well-structured data to generate realistic and compelling outputs. Here's a breakdown of key data preprocessing techniques for GANs:

1. Resizing and Cropping:

Standardization: Images in real-world datasets often come in various sizes. Resizing all images to a uniform size ensures consistent input for the GAN. Choose a resolution that captures sufficient detail while considering computational efficiency.

Cropping (Optional): Depending on your dataset and desired output, you might want to crop images to focus on specific regions of interest. For example, when training a GAN on facial images, you might crop to include only the face area, excluding irrelevant background details.

2. Normalization:

Pixel values in images typically range from 0 to 255 (for 8-bit grayscale images) or 0 to 255 for each color channel (RGB). However, GANs often work better with normalized data. Common normalization techniques include:

Scaling to [0, 1]: Divide each pixel value by 255. This brings all values into the range of 0 (black) to 1 (white) for grayscale images or 0 to 1 for each color channel (RGB).

Scaling to [-1, 1]: Subtract 127.5 from each pixel value and then divide by 127.5. This transforms the range to -1 (black) to 1 (white) for grayscale or -1 to 1 for each color channel (RGB).

3. Data Augmentation (Optional):

Data augmentation artificially expands your dataset by creating variations of existing images. This helps the GAN learn more robust features and become less susceptible to overfitting on the training data. Here are some common augmentation techniques:

Random Flipping: Flip images horizontally or vertically to introduce slight variations in pose or orientation.

Random Cropping: Randomly crop a portion of the image and resize it back to the original size. This exposes the GAN to different areas of the image and reduces the impact of specific image compositions.

Color Jittering: Randomly adjust brightness, contrast, saturation, and hue of the images to simulate lighting variations and enhance color diversity.

Rotation: Rotate images by random angles to introduce pose variations and prevent the GAN from learning specific orientations.

4. Class Imbalance (if applicable):

If your dataset contains imbalanced classes (e.g., significantly fewer images of a specific type), the GAN might prioritize learning the more frequent classes. To address this:
Oversampling: Duplicate images from the underrepresented classes to increase their presence in the training data.
Undersampling: Randomly remove images from the overrepresented classes to achieve a more balanced distribution.

5. Data Cleaning:

Real-world datasets might contain corrupted images, missing values, or outliers. These can negatively impact the training process. Here's how to handle them:
Identify and remove: Remove corrupted images or images with missing information if they constitute a small portion of the dataset.

Imputation: Fill in missing values using techniques like mean/median imputation or more sophisticated methods based on the data type.

Outlier removal: Consider removing extreme outliers if they significantly deviate from the overall distribution and might mislead the GAN.

Additional Considerations:

The choice of preprocessing techniques depends on your specific dataset, the type of images you want to generate, and the capabilities of your hardware. Experiment with different techniques to see what works best for your project.

Data augmentation should be applied with caution. Too much augmentation can create unrealistic artifacts and hinder the training process.

Consider using existing libraries like TensorFlow's tf.image module or OpenCV for efficient image preprocessing tasks.

By implementing these data preprocessing techniques, you can significantly improve the quality of your training data and pave the way for your GAN to achieve superior performance in generating realistic and creative outputs.

5.2 Strategies for Data Augmentation

Data augmentation is a powerful tool in the GAN toolbox, enabling you to create more robust and versatile models. By artificially expanding your dataset with variations of existing images, you can significantly enhance the quality of your generated outputs. Here, we delve into various data augmentation strategies to empower your GAN training:

1. Geometric Transformations:

Random Cropping: Simulate variations in focus and composition by randomly cropping a portion of the image and resizing it back to the original size. This exposes the GAN to different aspects of the subject and prevents it from overfitting to specific image compositions. Techniques include:
Center Crop: Crop a square region from the center of the image.
Random Crop: Randomly select a rectangular region from the image.
Random Flipping: Introduce pose variations and challenge the GAN's directional biases by randomly flipping images horizontally (left-right) or vertically (up-down).

Rotation: Rotate images by random angles to expose the GAN to objects from different viewpoints and prevent it from learning specific orientations. Be mindful of the nature of your data. Excessive rotation might not be suitable for objects with a well-defined "up" direction (e.g., furniture).

2. Color Space Transformations:

Color Jittering: Simulate lighting variations and enhance color diversity by randomly adjusting the following properties of the image:
Brightness: Increase or decrease the overall brightness of the image.
Contrast: Enhance or reduce the contrast between colors in the image.
Saturation: Make colors more or less vivid.
Hue: Shift the overall hue of the image, essentially changing its dominant color.
Random Color Channel Swapping: For RGB images, randomly swap the order of the color channels (Red, Green, Blue) to introduce a subtle variation and encourage the GAN to learn color relationships independently.
3. Noise Injection:

Gaussian Noise: Add a small amount of random Gaussian noise to the image to simulate sensor noise or imperfections in the real world. This can help the GAN learn to handle slight variations in image quality.

Salt-and-Pepper Noise: Introduce random black and white pixels to simulate image corruption or dust. Use this technique cautiously, as excessive noise can hinder training.

4. Advanced Techniques (Consider with Caution):

Elastic Deformations: Apply small, random elastic deformations to the image to simulate stretching or bending effects. This can be particularly useful for datasets containing objects with deformable parts (e.g., clothing).

Cutout: Randomly replace a rectangular region of the image with a random patch from another part of the same image. This can encourage the GAN to learn more holistic representations and reduce overfitting to specific image details.

General Considerations:

The effectiveness of data augmentation techniques depends on your specific dataset and desired outcome. Experiment with different techniques and adjust the augmentation parameters to find the optimal balance for your project.

Start with a conservative approach and gradually increase the strength of augmentation as you observe the impact on the training process. Too much augmentation can create unrealistic artifacts and hinder training.

Consider the computational cost of data augmentation. Techniques like random cropping and flipping are relatively inexpensive, while elastic deformations might require more processing power.

By strategically incorporating data augmentation into your GAN training pipeline, you can unlock its full potential. Remember, the key lies in finding the right balance between introducing variations and maintaining realism. With these strategies, you'll be well on your way to generating high-quality and diverse outputs from your GAN!

Chapter 6

Training Best Practices and GAN Stability

GAN training can be a thrilling yet temperamental journey. While the potential for generating awe-inspiring outputs is undeniable, achieving stable and successful training requires careful consideration of best practices. Here, we explore key strategies to navigate this creative landscape:

1. Hyperparameter Tuning:

Hyperparameters, such as learning rates, batch sizes, and weight initialization values, significantly influence training dynamics. Experimentation is crucial. Tools like TensorBoard can help visualize training progress and identify areas for improvement.

Learning Rate: A commonly encountered challenge is setting an appropriate learning rate. Too high, and the training might become unstable, causing the models to oscillate and fail to converge. Too low, and training might become painfully slow. Start with a conservative learning rate and gradually increase it if necessary.

Batch Size: The batch size defines the number of images processed simultaneously during training. A larger batch size can improve training efficiency but might lead to vanishing gradients and limit the ability to capture fine details. A smaller batch size can offer more nuanced updates but might come with increased training time. Experiment with different batch sizes to find a suitable balance.

2. Model Architectures:

While the DCGAN architecture serves as a solid foundation, consider exploring more sophisticated network designs like Spectral Normalization GANs (SNGANs) or Progressive Growing GANs (ProGANs) for specific tasks. These architectures incorporate techniques to address challenges like vanishing gradients and mode collapse.

Weight Initialization: Initialize weights in your Generator and Discriminator using techniques like Xavier initialization or He initialization, which are specifically designed for neural networks with non-linear activation functions like ReLU or Leaky ReLU. This helps to prevent exploding or vanishing gradients during training.

3. Monitoring and Evaluation:

Closely monitor training progress throughout the process. Tools like TensorBoard provide valuable insights into loss values, gradient norms, and generated image samples.

Loss Values: Track both Generator and Discriminator losses. Ideally, the Discriminator loss should decrease as it learns to distinguish real from fake, while the Generator loss should decrease as it fools the Discriminator.

Generated Images: Regularly evaluate the quality of generated images. Look for signs of mode collapse (where the Generator gets stuck producing a limited set of outputs) or artifacts.

4. Additional Techniques:

Gradient Penalties: Techniques like the Gradient Penalty can help to enforce a Lipschitz constraint on the Discriminator, leading to smoother training dynamics and improved stability.

Label Smoothing: Introduce a small amount of noise (typically between 0 and 0.1) to the real labels during Discriminator training. This can help to prevent the Discriminator from becoming overconfident and improve the quality of generated images.

Remember:

There's no "one-size-fits-all" solution for GAN training. The optimal approach depends on your specific dataset, desired outcome, and hardware capabilities.

Be prepared to experiment and adjust various aspects like hyperparameters, model architectures, and training configurations.

Patience is key. Training a GAN can be a time-consuming process.

By incorporating these best practices and remaining vigilant during training, you'll significantly increase your chances of achieving stable and successful GAN training, ultimately unlocking the power of this remarkable technology to generate captivating and realistic outputs.

6.1 Hyperparameter Tuning for GANs

GAN training is an intricate dance between the Generator and the Discriminator, and hyperparameters act as the music that guides this performance. Choosing the right hyperparameter values can significantly impact the quality and stability of your training process. Here, we delve into the art (and science) of hyperparameter tuning for GANs:

1. Crucial Hyperparameters:

Learning Rate (α): This controls the magnitude of weight updates in both the Generator and Discriminator. A high learning rate can lead to unstable training with oscillating losses, while a low learning rate can cause slow convergence. It's often beneficial to start with a conservative learning rate and gradually increase it if needed.

Batch Size (B): This defines the number of images processed simultaneously during training. A larger batch size improves efficiency but might lead to vanishing gradients and limit the ability to capture fine details. A smaller batch size offers more nuanced updates but requires more training iterations. Experiment to find a suitable balance.

Optimizer: Popular choices include Adam, RMSprop, or their variants. The choice can influence training speed and stability. Consider the properties of each optimizer and its effectiveness for GAN training.

2. Additional Hyperparameters:

Network Architectures: While architectures like DCGAN provide a foundation, consider exploring options like Spectral Normalization GANs (SNGANs) or Progressive Growing GANs (ProGANs) for specific tasks. These might introduce their own hyperparameters related to weight normalization or progressive growth.

Weight Initialization: Techniques like Xavier or He initialization help prevent exploding or vanishing gradients. Some frameworks might offer additional hyperparameters for specific initialization methods.

Gradient Penalty (λ_gp): This penalty term (used in WGAN-GP) enforces a Lipschitz constraint on the Discriminator, promoting smoother training dynamics. The value of λ_gp can be tuned for optimal results.

3. Strategies for Hyperparameter Tuning:

Grid Search: This exhaustive approach systematically evaluates combinations of hyperparameter values. While comprehensive, it can be computationally expensive for a large number of hyperparameters.

Random Search: This method randomly samples hyperparameter values from defined ranges. It's less computationally intensive but might miss optimal configurations.

Bayesian Optimization: This advanced approach uses past evaluations to guide the search for promising hyperparameter combinations. It can be efficient but requires more complex implementation.

4. Tools and Techniques:

TensorBoard: Visualize training progress, including loss values, gradient norms, and generated image samples. This helps identify areas for improvement and assess the impact of hyperparameter changes.

Early Stopping: Implement a mechanism to stop training if progress stagnates or loss values diverge for a certain number of epochs. This prevents wasted computation time.

Learning Rate Decay: Gradually decrease the learning rate over time. This can help the model converge more precisely in later training stages.

5. Remember:

There's no "golden set" of hyperparameters for all GANs. The optimal configuration depends on your specific dataset, desired outcome, and hardware capabilities.

Be prepared for an iterative process. Experiment with different hyperparameter combinations, evaluate the results, and refine your approach based on your observations.

Utilize available tools and techniques like those mentioned above to streamline the hyperparameter tuning process and accelerate your journey to successful GAN training.

By mastering the art of hyperparameter tuning, you'll unlock the full potential of your GANs, enabling them to generate stunningly realistic and creative outputs. So, experiment, iterate, and witness the magic unfold!

6.2 Addressing Mode Collapse and Training Issues

,GANs, with their ability to generate realistic and creative content, hold immense potential. However, their training journey can be fraught with challenges, particularly the dreaded mode collapse. This phenomenon occurs when the Generator becomes fixated on producing a limited set of outputs, neglecting the rich diversity present in the training data. It's like an artist stuck in a creative rut, churning out repetitive variations of the same theme.

Here, we delve into practical strategies to combat mode collapse and ensure your GAN training flourishes:

Understanding Mode Collapse:

Imagine training a GAN on a dataset of diverse faces. Ideally, the Generator should learn to produce a variety of faces reflecting different ages, ethnicities, and expressions. But in mode collapse, the Generator might get stuck on a narrow subset, repeatedly generating faces with a similar appearance. This significantly limits the creative potential of the GAN.

Early Detection is Key:

Visual Inspection: Regularly assess the quality and diversity of generated images throughout training. Look for signs of repetitive patterns or a lack of variation in features. Tools like TensorBoard can help visualize generated samples at different training stages.

Quantitative Metrics: While visual inspection is crucial, consider using metrics like Inception Score (IS) or Fréchet Inception Distance (FID) to measure the quality and diversity of generated images. These metrics compare the

generated data distribution to the real data distribution, with higher scores indicating better performance.
Combating Mode Collapse:

Diversity-Promoting Techniques:

Minibatch Discrimination: Instead of feeding the Discriminator with isolated images, present it with additional information about the minibatch it's evaluating. This could involve minibatch statistics like mean or standard deviation, or encouraging the Discriminator to consider relationships between images within the minibatch. This challenges the Discriminator to look beyond easily replicated features and forces the Generator to explore a broader range of outputs.

Spectral Normalization (SNGAN): Apply spectral normalization to the weights of the Discriminator's convolutional layers. This technique helps prevent vanishing gradients, a common culprit in mode collapse. By maintaining healthy gradients, the Discriminator can provide more informative feedback to the Generator, guiding it towards diverse outputs.

Regularization:

Weight Decay: Introduce a penalty term during training that discourages the Generator and Discriminator from having excessively large weights. This helps to prevent overfitting to specific features in the training data and encourages the models to learn more generalizable representations, ultimately leading to a wider range of generated outputs.

Dropout: Randomly drop out a certain percentage of activations during training in both the Generator and Discriminator. This prevents the models from becoming overly reliant on specific features and forces them to learn more robust representations, promoting diversity in the generated outputs.

Addressing Training Issues:

Gradients:

Vanishing Gradients: If the Discriminator becomes too good at classifying real images, the Generator might receive weak or vanishing gradients during backpropagation. This hinders the Generator's ability to learn and improve. Techniques like leaky ReLU activation functions or weight normalization (like spectral normalization) can help to address this by allowing gradients to flow more effectively through the network.

Training Dynamics:

Unbalanced Training: Ensure a balance in the difficulty of tasks presented to the Discriminator. If real images are significantly easier to classify than fake images, the

Discriminator might lose motivation to improve. This can lead to the Generator getting stuck in a rut. Techniques like label smoothing can help to address this. Label smoothing involves adding a small amount of noise (typically between 0 and 0.1) to the real labels during Discriminator training. This injects some uncertainty into the training process, preventing the Discriminator from becoming overconfident and allowing the Generator to continue learning and exploring the data distribution.

Early Stopping: Implement a mechanism to stop training if progress stagnates or loss values diverge for a certain number of epochs. This prevents wasted computation time and allows you to intervene and adjust hyperparameters or training configurations if necessary.

Practical Implementation Tips:

Code Snippet (PyTorch): Here's a basic PyTorch code example demonstrating minibatch discrimination using mean features:

Python
import torch

```python
def minibatch_discrimination(real_data, fake_data):
  # Calculate mean features for real and fake minibatch
  real_mean = torch.mean(real_data, dim=0, keepdim=True)
  fake_mean = torch.mean(fake_data, dim=0, keepdim=True)
  # Concatenate real and fake features
  combined_features = torch.cat([real_mean, fake_mean], dim=1)
  return combined_features
```

Use code with caution.

content_copy

This code snippet calculates the mean features for both the real and fake

we can integrate minibatch discrimination into the Discriminator:

Python
import torch

```python
def discriminator(x, features):
  # ... (Your existing Discriminator architecture)
  # Add a layer to process the combined features
```

```
    x = torch.cat([x, features], dim=1)  # Concatenate image
features and minibatch features
    # ... (Continue with your Discriminator architecture)
    return output

def train_step(real_images, noise):
    # ... (Your existing training loop logic)
    # Calculate minibatch features
        features  =  minibatch_discrimination(real_images,
fake_images)
    # Pass features to the Discriminator
    real_loss = discriminator_loss(discriminator(real_images,
features))
    fake_loss = discriminator_loss(discriminator(fake_images,
features))
    # ... (Continue with your training loop logic)
```

Use code with caution.

content_copy

In this modified training loop, the minibatch_discrimination function calculates the mean features for both real and fake images. These features are then concatenated with the image features before feeding them into the Discriminator. This allows the Discriminator to consider not only the individual images but also the relationships between images within the minibatch, promoting diversity in the generated outputs.

Additional Practical Considerations:

Hyperparameter Tuning: Experiment with different hyperparameter values, such as the learning rate, batch size, and weight decay coefficients. These can significantly impact training dynamics and the susceptibility to mode collapse. Tools like TensorBoard can help you visualize the impact of hyperparameter changes on training progress and generated image quality.

Gradient Penalty (WGAN-GP): Consider using the Gradient Penalty (λ_gp) term introduced in WGAN-GP. This penalty term enforces a Lipschitz constraint on the Discriminator, which can help to stabilize training and prevent mode collapse.

Alternative Architectures: Explore architectures like Progressive Growing GANs (ProGANs) that are specifically designed to address mode collapse and generate high-resolution images. These architectures often incorporate techniques like progressive training and minibatch striding to encourage the Generator to learn to produce increasingly detailed and diverse outputs.

Remember:

There's no "one-size-fits-all" solution to combat mode collapse. The optimal approach depends on your specific dataset, desired outcome, and hardware capabilities. However, by implementing the strategies outlined above, closely monitoring your training process, and being prepared to adapt your approach, you can significantly increase your chances of achieving successful and diverse GAN training.

Part 4: Evaluating and Deploying GANs

Chapter 7
Evaluating GAN Performance

Training a GAN is an intricate dance between the Generator and the Discriminator, and gauging their success requires a multi-faceted approach. Here, we delve into key metrics and techniques to effectively evaluate your GAN's performance:

Understanding the Challenge:

Evaluating GANs presents a unique challenge. Unlike standard classification or regression models, there's no single, definitive metric to declare victory. A GAN's performance hinges on a delicate balance between two key aspects:

Fidelity (Image Quality): How realistic and visually appealing are the generated images?
Diversity: Does the GAN produce a wide variety of outputs that capture the essence of the training data distribution?
Metrics for Fidelity:

Inception Score (IS): This metric leverages a pre-trained image classification model (like Inception v3) to assess the quality of generated images. Higher IS scores indicate better fidelity, with the generated images likely to be classified correctly by the pre-trained model.

Fréchet Inception Distance (FID): FID measures the distance between the distributions of real and generated images in a feature space extracted from a pre-trained model. Lower FID scores indicate a closer match between the real and generated data distributions, suggesting higher image quality.

Metrics for Diversity:

Inception Score (IS): While also indicative of fidelity, IS can also indirectly reflect diversity. A high IS often implies a variety of realistic outputs being generated.

Nearest Neighbor Analysis: This technique involves comparing generated images to the nearest neighbors in the training data. A diverse set of generated images will have neighbors scattered throughout the training data, indicating they explore different regions of the data distribution.

Additional Considerations:

Human Evaluation: While metrics provide valuable insights, subjective human evaluation remains crucial. Assess the generated images for realism, coherence, and adherence to the desired style or theme of your project.

Task-Specific Metrics: If your GAN is designed for a specific task (e.g., generating realistic textures for a 3D scene), consider metrics relevant to that task. For example, you might evaluate the quality of generated textures by incorporating them into a 3D rendering engine and assessing their visual appeal within the scene.

Techniques and Best Practices:

Visual Sampling: Regularly evaluate generated images throughout training to monitor progress and identify potential issues like mode collapse (limited output diversity).

TensorBoard Integration: Leverage tools like TensorBoard to visualize training metrics (loss values, IS, FID) and generated image samples at different training stages. This allows you to track progress and identify areas for improvement.

Inception Network Scores: Utilize pre-trained Inception networks to calculate IS and FID. These metrics provide valuable insights into the quality and diversity of your generated outputs.

Comparison with Baseline: Compare the performance of your GAN to a baseline model (e.g., random noise generation). This helps to highlight the effectiveness of your GAN in learning the underlying data distribution.

Remember:

The optimal evaluation strategy depends on your specific goals and application. Consider a combination of metrics, human evaluation, and task-specific considerations to gain a comprehensive understanding of your GAN's performance. By effectively evaluating your GAN, you can refine your training process and unlock its full potential to generate captivating and diverse outputs.

7.1 Quantitative Metrics for GAN Evaluation

GANs, with their ability to conjure realistic and creative content, have revolutionized various fields. But assessing their success goes beyond a simple "wow" factor. Quantitative metrics offer valuable insights into a GAN's performance, guiding you towards optimal training and impressive outputs. Here, we delve into key metrics to evaluate your GAN's journey:

Fidelity: How Real Are Those Pixels?

Fidelity refers to the visual quality and realism of the generated images. Here are metrics that shed light on this aspect:

Inception Score (IS): This metric leverages a pre-trained image classification model (like Inception v3). The model assigns class labels (e.g., "cat," "dog") to both real and generated images. A high IS score indicates that the generated images are not only realistic but also classified correctly by the pre-trained model, suggesting they capture the essence of real-world categories.

Fréchet Inception Distance (FID): FID measures the distance between the distributions of real and generated images in a feature space extracted from a pre-trained model like Inception. Imagine a high-dimensional landscape where each data point represents an image. FID calculates the difference between the distribution of real image features and the distribution of generated image features in this space. Lower FID scores indicate a closer match between the real and generated data distributions, suggesting higher image fidelity.

Diversity: Beyond Monotony - Exploring the Spectrum

Diversity refers to the variety of outputs a GAN can produce. A good GAN shouldn't get stuck in a rut, churning out repetitive images. These metrics help assess this:

Inception Score (IS) (Yes, it plays a dual role!): While IS is indicative of fidelity, it can also indirectly reflect diversity. A high IS often implies that the model isn't just producing a few very realistic images, but a variety of realistic outputs, thus capturing the breadth of the training data distribution.

Nearest Neighbor Analysis: This technique involves comparing generated images to their closest neighbors in the training data. Diverse generated images will have neighbors scattered throughout the training data space, indicating they explore different regions of the data distribution. Conversely, images with poor diversity will tend to have neighbors clustered together, suggesting they haven't ventured far from a limited set of patterns.

Additional Considerations:

Metrics are a Tool, Not the Truth: While metrics provide valuable guidance, they shouldn't be the sole arbiter of success. Human evaluation remains crucial. Assess the generated images for visual quality, coherence, and adherence to the desired style or theme of your project.

Task-Specific Considerations: If your GAN is designed for a specific task (e.g., generating realistic textures for a 3D scene), consider metrics relevant to that task. For example, you might evaluate the quality of generated textures by incorporating them into a 3D rendering engine and assessing their visual appeal within the scene.

Remember:

The optimal evaluation strategy depends on your specific goals and application. Don't get hung up on a single metric. Instead, use a combination of approaches – quantitative metrics, human evaluation, and task-specific considerations – to gain a well-rounded understanding of your GAN's performance. By effectively wielding these tools, you can steer your GAN training towards generating captivatingly diverse and realistic outputs.

7.2 Qualitative Assessment of Generated Samples

While quantitative metrics provide valuable insights into a GAN's performance, they can't capture the full picture. The human eye excels at detecting subtleties and nuances that metrics might miss. Qualitative assessment of generated samples is essential for a holistic evaluation of your GAN's creative prowess. Here's how to harness this powerful tool:

What to Look For:

Visual Quality: Assess the overall realism and coherence of the generated images. Do they appear believable and free of artifacts or unnatural blurring?

Style and Theme: Are the generated images consistent with the desired style or theme of your project? For example, if you're training a GAN on portraits, do the generated faces capture the essence of human portraiture?

Diversity: Do the generated images exhibit a variety of styles, compositions, and details? Or do they fall into a limited set of repetitive patterns?

Internal Consistency: Within each generated image, are there any inconsistencies or logical flaws? For example, does a person have two left hands, or does a landscape have nonsensical lighting?

Emotional Impact: Does the generated content evoke any emotions in the viewer? This might be particularly relevant for projects aiming to create artistic or evocative outputs.

Techniques for Qualitative Assessment:

Visual Inspection: Regularly evaluate generated images throughout training. This allows you to monitor progress, identify potential issues like mode collapse (limited diversity), and make adjustments to the training process as needed.

Side-by-Side Comparisons: Compare generated images to real images from your training data. This helps to identify how closely the generated images resemble the real data distribution.

Human Rating Studies: Conduct studies where human subjects evaluate the quality, diversity, and other aspects of the generated images. This provides valuable insights from a diverse set of perspectives.

Additional Considerations:

Domain Expertise: If your GAN is generating content in a specific domain (e.g., medical images, architectural models), consider involving domain experts in the qualitative assessment process. They can provide valuable insights based on their knowledge of the specific domain.

Documentation: Keep a record of the qualitative assessment process, including notes on observed issues, successful outputs, and areas for improvement. This documentation can be invaluable for future reference and refinement of your GAN training process.

Remember:

Qualitative assessment is an iterative process. As your GAN training progresses, your expectations and criteria for evaluation might evolve. Don't be afraid to adapt your approach based on the evolving capabilities of your GAN and the specific goals of your project.

By effectively combining quantitative metrics with qualitative assessment, you can gain a comprehensive understanding of your GAN's performance and guide it towards generating not just realistic but also captivating and diverse outputs that fulfill the artistic vision of your project.

Chapter 8

Deploying GAN Models for Real-world Applications

GANs have transcended the realm of research labs and are now poised to revolutionize various industries. But the journey from a well-trained GAN to a real-world application requires careful consideration. Here, we delve into practical strategies for deploying GAN models and unlocking their potential:

Understanding Deployment Challenges:

Computational Demands: Running a GAN for inference (generating images) can be computationally expensive, especially for high-resolution outputs. This necessitates optimizing the model for efficient deployment on specific hardware platforms.

Latency Considerations: In real-time applications, latency (the time it takes to generate an image) is crucial. Techniques like model quantization and pruning can help to reduce latency without compromising image quality.

Integration with Existing Systems: Deploying a GAN often involves integrating it with existing software or hardware infrastructure. Consider factors like data pipelines, API design, and compatibility with other systems.

Scalability: If your application expects high volumes of image generation requests, ensure your deployment architecture can handle increased load without performance degradation.

Planning for Deployment:

Define Use Case: Clearly define the specific real-world application for your GAN. This will guide decisions about model optimization, hardware selection, and integration strategies.

Hardware Selection: Consider the trade-off between computational power, cost, and power consumption. Popular options include GPUs, TPUs, and specialized AI accelerators. Tools like NVIDIA's TensorRT can help optimize models for specific hardware platforms.

Model Optimization: Techniques like model pruning, quantization, and knowledge distillation can significantly reduce model size and computational footprint, making them more suitable for deployment on resource-constrained devices.

Deployment Strategies:

Stand-alone Application: Deploy the GAN as a stand-alone application that users can interact with directly. This might be suitable for internal use cases or research purposes.

API Integration: Develop an API (Application Programming Interface) that allows other applications to interact with your GAN and request image generation. This facilitates integration with existing workflows and broader adoption.

Cloud-based Deployment: Leverage cloud platforms like Google Cloud AI Platform or Amazon SageMaker to deploy your GAN. Cloud platforms offer scalable infrastructure, pre-built tools for model management, and easy access to powerful computing resources.

Practical Considerations:

Containerization: Package your GAN model and its dependencies (libraries, frameworks) into a container using tools like Docker. This simplifies deployment across different environments and ensures consistent behavior.

Monitoring and Logging: Implement monitoring and logging mechanisms to track the performance of your deployed GAN. This allows you to identify potential issues like errors, performance bottlenecks, or data drift.

Version Control: Maintain good version control practices for your GAN code and deployment configuration. This allows you to track changes, revert to previous versions if necessary, and streamline the deployment process.
Case Studies and Examples:

Fashion Industry: GANs can be used to generate realistic images of clothing items on models in different poses. This reduces the need for expensive photoshoots and allows for faster product exploration and design iteration. (Implementation Example: StyleGAN2 for generating high-fidelity clothing images on different body types)
Media and Entertainment: GANs can be used to create realistic special effects, generate personalized avatars, or even create realistic trailers for upcoming movies based on scripts. (Implementation Example: Deep Video Portraits for generating animated facial expressions on existing portraits)

Drug Discovery: GANs can be used to generate novel molecular structures for potential drug candidates, accelerating the drug discovery process. (Implementation Example: MoleculeGAN for generating new molecules with desired properties)

Remember:

Deploying a GAN successfully requires a holistic approach. By carefully considering the computational demands, defining your use case, selecting the right hardware and deployment strategy, and implementing best practices, you can transform your GAN from a research project to a powerful tool that drives innovation in your chosen field. As you gain experience, don't hesitate to experiment with different deployment strategies and continuously refine your approach to unlock the full potential of GANs in the real world.

8.1 TensorFlow Serving for Model Deployment

Having trained a powerful GAN, you're ready to unleash its creative potential in real-world applications. TensorFlow Serving (TF Serving) emerges as a robust and versatile platform to seamlessly deploy your GAN for efficient image generation. Here's how TF Serving empowers your GAN deployment journey:

Understanding TensorFlow Serving:

TF Serving is an open-source framework developed by Google for serving machine learning models. It acts as a bridge between your trained GAN model and various client applications, enabling them to interact with the model and request image generation.

Benefits of Using TF Serving for GAN Deployment:

Simplified Deployment: TF Serving streamlines the deployment process by providing a standardized way to serve models. You can package your GAN model along with its dependencies, making it easier to deploy across different environments.

Scalability: TF Serving is designed to handle high volumes of requests efficiently. This is crucial for real-world applications where your GAN might need to generate images for multiple users concurrently.

Flexibility: TF Serving supports various model formats, including TensorFlow SavedModels, commonly used for GANs. It also offers multiple serving options like REST API and gRPC, allowing you to choose the most suitable method for your application.

Versioning: TF Serving allows you to manage different versions of your GAN model. This enables you to experiment with different training configurations or deploy improved versions of the model without disrupting ongoing applications.

Steps for Deploying a GAN with TF Serving:

Save Your GAN Model: Use TensorFlow's SavedModel format to save your trained GAN. This format encapsulates the model architecture, weights, and any additional assets needed for inference (image generation).

Prepare the Serving Environment: Set up a server environment to host TF Serving. This could be a local machine, a cloud instance, or a containerized environment using Docker.

Configure TF Serving: Use TF Serving APIs to configure how your GAN model will be served. This typically involves specifying the model location, preferred serving options (REST API or gRPC), and any required pre-processing or post-processing steps.

Start the TF Serving Server: Launch the TF Serving server on your chosen environment. This makes your GAN model accessible for client applications.

Develop Client Applications: Build client applications that interact with the TF Serving server. Clients can send requests containing noise vectors or other input parameters, and TF Serving will use your GAN model to generate the corresponding images.

Additional Considerations:

Model Optimization: Before deployment, consider techniques like model pruning or quantization to reduce the model size and computational footprint. This can be particularly important if you're deploying on resource-constrained hardware.

Security: Implement security measures to restrict unauthorized access to your deployed GAN model. This might involve authentication and authorization mechanisms for client applications.

Monitoring and Logging: Monitor the performance of your deployed GAN using tools provided by TF Serving. This allows you to identify potential issues like errors, high latency, or unexpected resource usage.

Benefits Beyond Deployment:

Standardization: TF Serving promotes a standardized approach to model deployment, making it easier to integrate your GAN with other machine learning models or existing workflows.

Flexibility: TF Serving's support for various model formats and serving options allows you to adapt your deployment strategy based on your specific needs and infrastructure.

By leveraging TensorFlow Serving, you can transform your GAN from a research project to a powerful and accessible tool. This bridge between your model and the real world empowers you to unlock the creative potential of GANs and drive innovation in various fields.

8.2 Integrating GANs into Web and Mobile Applications

GANs have revolutionized image generation, offering boundless possibilities for web and mobile applications. But integrating these powerful models requires careful planning and execution. Here, we delve into practical strategies to seamlessly integrate GANs into your web and mobile apps:

Understanding the Challenges:

Computational Demands: Generating high-resolution images with GANs can be computationally expensive. This can lead to performance issues, especially on mobile devices with limited resources.

Latency Considerations: For real-time interactive applications, the time it takes for the GAN to generate an image (latency) is crucial. Techniques like model optimization and efficient data transfer are essential.

Security: Mitigate potential security risks associated with user-provided input. Malicious users might try to manipulate the GAN to generate harmful content.

API Design: For web applications, design an intuitive and efficient API that allows clients to interact with the GAN and request image generation.

Planning for Integration:

Define Use Case: Clearly define how your GAN will be used within the application. This will guide decisions about model selection, optimization strategies, and user interface design.

Model Selection: Consider the trade-off between image quality and computational efficiency. For mobile applications, a smaller, optimized version of your GAN might be necessary. Tools like TensorFlow Lite for mobile deployment can be helpful.

Frontend Design: Design a user-friendly interface that allows users to interact with the GAN. This might involve providing controls for input parameters, noise injection, or style selection.

Integration Strategies:

Server-side Deployment: Deploy your GAN model on a server with sufficient computational resources. Web applications can then interact with the GAN through an API, offloading the image generation task from the client's device. This approach ensures smooth performance even on less powerful devices.

WebAssembly (WASM): Explore deploying a lightweight version of your GAN model to WebAssembly. WASM allows running compiled code (often from languages like C++) within web browsers, enabling more efficient image generation on the client-side. This approach can reduce latency but might require more upfront effort for model conversion.

Hybrid Approach: Combine server-side deployment with client-side processing. The client can handle tasks like noise vector generation or basic image pre-processing, while the server performs the computationally intensive image generation using the full GAN model.

Practical Considerations:

Model Optimization: Apply techniques like model pruning, quantization, or knowledge distillation to reduce the model size and computational footprint. This is crucial for both server-side and client-side deployments.

Data Transfer Optimization: Optimize data transfer between the client application and the server (if using server-side deployment). Techniques like image compression or efficient data serialization can minimize network bandwidth usage.

Security Measures: Implement robust input validation and sanitization mechanisms to prevent users from injecting malicious code or manipulating the GAN to generate inappropriate content.

Offline Functionality (Mobile): For mobile applications, consider enabling basic functionalities even when offline. This could involve pre-generating a set of images or allowing users to manipulate previously generated outputs.

Libraries and Frameworks:

TensorFlow.js: A JavaScript library from TensorFlow that enables running machine learning models in web browsers. This can be helpful for client-side GAN integration using WebAssembly.

PyTorch Mobile: A framework for deploying PyTorch models on mobile devices. It offers tools for model optimization and deployment to platforms like Android and iOS.

Case Studies and Examples:

Image Editing Applications: Integrate a GAN model to offer users real-time image editing features like style transfer, color correction, or background removal. (Implementation Example: StyleGAN for real-time style transfer effects on user-uploaded images)

AI-powered Avatars: Develop an application that allows users to create personalized avatars using a GAN. Users can provide input parameters like facial features, clothing style, or pose to generate unique and realistic avatars.

(Implementation Example: StyleGAN2 for generating high-fidelity avatars based on user-specified attributes)

Augmented Reality Experiences: Utilize a GAN to generate realistic objects or environments for augmented reality (AR) applications. This can enhance the user experience by providing immersive and interactive AR experiences. (Implementation Example: Pix2Pix for generating realistic 3D objects from user-provided sketches)

Remember:

Integrating GANs into web and mobile applications requires a balance between functionality, performance, and security. By carefully considering the use case, selecting the right deployment strategy, and optimizing your model and application, you can unlock the power of GANs to create innovative and engaging user experiences. As the field of GANs continues to evolve, the possibilities for creative integration into web and mobile applications will only become

Part 5: Advanced GAN Techniques (Optional)

Chapter 9
Exploring Conditional GANs (cGANs)

'

While Generative Adversarial Networks (GANs) have revolutionized image generation, their outputs can sometimes lack specific characteristics. Enter Conditional GANs (cGANs), a powerful extension that injects control and direction into the generation process. Here, we delve into the world of cGANs and unlock their potential for creating tailored and diverse outputs.

Understanding cGANs:

Imagine a regular GAN as an artist limited to painting portraits. A cGAN, on the other hand, is like an artist who can be given specific instructions – "paint a portrait of a woman with red hair and a smiling expression." cGANs achieve this control by incorporating conditioning information into the training process. This information guides the Generator towards producing images that adhere to the specified conditions.

How cGANs Work:

Conditional Inputs: cGANs introduce additional input alongside the random noise vector typically used by GANs. This additional input can take various forms, such as class labels (e.g., "cat," "dog"), text descriptions, or even images representing the desired style.

Modified Architectures: The cGAN architecture is modified to incorporate the conditioning information. This often involves feeding the conditional input to both the Generator and the Discriminator. The Generator uses this information to steer its image generation process, while the Discriminator learns to evaluate images based on both their realism and adherence to the conditions.

Benefits of cGANs:

Targeted Image Generation: cGANs allow you to generate images with specific attributes or styles. This is particularly useful for applications like creating product variations, generating images based on user descriptions, or translating images from one style to another (e.g., sketch to photo).

Improved Diversity: cGANs can help mitigate mode collapse, a common issue in vanilla GANs where the Generator gets stuck producing a limited set of outputs. By providing specific conditions, you can encourage the

Generator to explore a wider range of possibilities within the defined constraints.

Creative Exploration: cGANs open doors for creative exploration. You can experiment with different conditioning information to discover new aesthetics or generate unexpected combinations of styles.

Exploring cGAN Applications:

Fashion Industry: Generate clothing variations based on style, color, or size using conditioning information.

Art and Design: Create unique artwork by combining different artistic styles or generating images based on textual descriptions.

Medical Imaging: Synthesize realistic medical images with specific pathologies for training and research purposes.

Examples of cGAN Architectures:

ACGAN (Auxiliary Classifier GAN): A popular cGAN architecture where the conditioning information is fed into an additional classifier network that assists the Discriminator in evaluating image authenticity and adherence to the condition.

InfoGAN: This cGAN variant aims to learn a latent representation of the conditioning information, allowing for more efficient encoding and potentially more diverse outputs.

Remember:

cGANs are a powerful tool, but they require careful consideration during training. Here are some additional points to keep in mind:

Choosing the Right Conditioning Information: The effectiveness of a cGAN hinges on the quality and relevance of the conditioning information provided. Ensure the information is clear, well-defined, and aligns with the desired outputs.
Training Challenges: Training cGANs can be more complex compared to vanilla GANs due to the additional layer of complexity introduced by the conditioning information. Techniques like careful hyperparameter tuning and monitoring training progress are crucial for successful training.

By harnessing the power of cGANs, you can unlock a new level of control and direction in your image generation tasks. From creating targeted content to exploring creative possibilities, cGANs offer a gateway to a more versatile and impactful future of Generative Adversarial Networks.

9.1 Generating Targeted Outputs with cGANs

While Generative Adversarial Networks (GANs) have become synonymous with impressive image generation, their vanilla form can sometimes lack precise control. Enter Conditional GANs (cGANs), a powerful upgrade that injects a dose of directionality into the generation process. Here, we explore how cGANs empower you to craft highly targeted and diverse outputs, tailored to your specific needs.

Unleashing Specificity:

Imagine a standard GAN as a painter limited to landscapes. A cGAN, on the other hand, is like an artist who can be given specific instructions – "paint a landscape of a lush green forest at sunrise with a winding river flowing through it." cGANs achieve this focused output by incorporating conditioning information into the training process. This information acts as a guiding light for the Generator, directing it towards producing images that adhere to the specified criteria.

The Mechanics Behind the Magic:

Conditional Inputs: cGANs introduce an additional layer of input alongside the usual random noise vector fed to standard GANs. This conditioning information can take various forms, including:

Class labels: Categorical data like "cat," "dog," or "furniture" can guide the Generator to produce images belonging to specific classes.

Text descriptions: Detailed descriptions like "a close-up portrait of a smiling woman with red hair and freckles" provide a rich source of conditioning information for the Generator.

Images: Existing images representing a desired style or theme can be used to condition the GAN, allowing it to generate variations or new images that adhere to that style.

Modified Architectures: The cGAN architecture is tweaked to accommodate the conditioning information. This often involves feeding the conditional input to both the Generator and the Discriminator. The Generator leverages this information to steer its image creation process, while the Discriminator learns to assess images based on two key aspects:

Realism: How realistic and believable is the generated image?
Condition Adherence: Does the image adhere to the specified conditions or capture the essence of the conditioning information?
Benefits of Targeted Generation with cGANs:

Precision and Control: cGANs empower you to generate images with specific attributes or styles. This is a game-changer for applications like:

Product Design: Generate variations of clothing items based on style, color, or size.

Image Editing: Create targeted edits like changing the background of an image or adding specific objects.
Text-to-Image Synthesis: Translate textual descriptions into corresponding images, opening doors for creative exploration.

Combating Mode Collapse: A common challenge in vanilla GANs is mode collapse, where the Generator gets stuck producing a limited set of outputs. cGANs, by providing specific conditions, nudge the Generator to explore a wider range of possibilities within the defined constraints, promoting greater diversity in the generated outputs.

Unlocking Creative Potential: cGANs are a springboard for creative exploration. Experiment with different conditioning information to discover new artistic styles, generate unexpected combinations of elements, or produce variations on a theme.

Exploring Applications of Targeted Generation:

Fashion Industry: Create clothing designs with variations in style, color, or pattern based on user preferences or seasonal trends.

Art and Design: Generate unique artwork by combining different artistic styles or translating user sketches into realistic paintings.

Media and Entertainment: Personalize video game characters with user-defined appearances or create trailers for upcoming movies based on script descriptions.

Popular cGAN Architectures for Targeted Generation:

ACGAN (Auxiliary Classifier GAN): A widely used cGAN architecture where the conditioning information is fed into an additional classifier network. This network assists the Discriminator in evaluating image authenticity and adherence to the condition.

InfoGAN: This cGAN variant aims to learn a latent representation of the conditioning information. This compressed encoding can lead to more efficient training and potentially more diverse outputs within the specified conditions.

Remember:

While cGANs offer immense power for targeted generation, they require thoughtful considerations during training:

Choosing the Right Conditioning Information: The effectiveness of a cGAN hinges on the quality and relevance of the conditioning information provided. Ensure the information is clear, well-defined, and aligns with the desired outputs.

Training Nuances: Training cGANs can be more intricate compared to vanilla GANs due to the added layer of complexity from the conditioning information. Techniques like careful hyperparameter tuning and close monitoring of training progress are crucial for successful training.

By harnessing the power of cGANs, you can move beyond generic image generation and delve into a world of targeted creativity. From crafting highly specific outputs to exploring uncharted artistic territories, cGANs empower you to push the

9.2 Applications of Conditional GANs

Conditional Generative Adversarial Networks (cGANs) have emerged as a powerful extension of the image generation revolution spearheaded by GANs. Unlike their vanilla counterparts, cGANs offer a crucial element of control, allowing you to steer the generation process towards targeted outputs. This newfound ability unlocks a vast array of applications across diverse fields. Let's delve into some of the most exciting ways cGANs are transforming various industries:

Crafting with Precision:

Fashion Design: Imagine generating endless variations of clothing items based on user preferences. cGANs can create new designs with specified styles (e.g., casual, formal), colors, or patterns. This empowers fashion houses to explore design possibilities, personalize clothing for customers, and optimize product offerings for different markets.

Product Design: Similar to fashion, cGANs can be used to generate variations of furniture pieces, electronic devices, or other products with specific features or functionalities. This allows designers to experiment with different design elements, rapidly prototype variations, and cater to diverse customer needs.

Bridging the Gap Between Text and Image:

Text-to-Image Synthesis: cGANs can bridge the gap between textual descriptions and corresponding images. Imagine describing a "fantasy landscape with a majestic waterfall cascading into a crystal-clear lake" and witnessing the cGAN bring your words to life. This opens doors for applications like generating illustrations for children's books, creating concept art based on story descriptions, or even personalizing marketing materials with targeted imagery.

Image Editing and Manipulation:

Targeted Image Editing: cGANs can be used to make specific edits to existing images. Want to change the background of a photo, add a missing object, or adjust the lighting? cGANs can handle these tasks while ensuring the edits seamlessly blend into the original image, preserving its overall quality and realism.

Style Transfer: Imagine applying the artistic style of Van Gogh to a photograph. cGANs can achieve this by learning the essence of a particular style from reference images and then applying it to new content. This opens doors for creative photo editing, generating artistic variations of existing photographs, or even personalizing artwork based on user preferences.

Augmenting Realities:

Augmented Reality (AR) Content Creation: cGANs can generate realistic 3D objects or environments for AR applications. This can be particularly useful for creating immersive and interactive AR experiences in areas like product visualization, educational simulations, or even personalized AR filters for social media.

Beyond the Obvious:

Medical Imaging: cGANs have the potential to synthesize realistic medical images with specific pathologies. This can be invaluable for training medical professionals, developing new diagnostic tools, or even personalizing treatment plans. Drug Discovery: By generating novel molecular structures with desired properties, cGANs can accelerate the drug discovery process, leading to the development of new life-saving medications.

Exploring the Nuances:

These are just a few examples of the vast potential cGANs hold. As the technology continues to evolve, we can expect even more innovative applications to emerge. However, it's important to remember:

Data Quality Matters: The quality and relevance of the conditioning information significantly impact the outputs. Ensure your conditioning data is clear, well-defined, and aligns with the desired outcomes.

Training Challenges: Training cGANs can be more intricate than vanilla GANs due to the added layer of complexity from the conditioning information. Careful hyperparameter tuning and close monitoring of the training process are crucial for success.

In Conclusion:

cGANs represent a significant leap forward in the realm of image generation. By introducing the element of control, they empower us to generate highly targeted and diverse outputs, pushing the boundaries of creativity and innovation across a multitude of fields. As we continue to explore the potential of cGANs, the possibilities for creating tailored and impactful content seem limitless.

Chapter 10

State-of-the-Art GAN Architectures (e.g., StyleGAN)

Generative Adversarial Networks (GANs) have revolutionized image generation, but the quest for ever-more impressive and realistic outputs continues. At the forefront of this pursuit lie cutting-edge GAN architectures like StyleGAN, pushing the boundaries of what's possible. Here, we delve into these architectural marvels, exploring their inner workings and the remarkable results they produce.

Understanding the Need for New Architectures:

Early GANs, while groundbreaking, faced limitations. Issues like mode collapse (getting stuck generating a limited set of images) and difficulty in controlling image style hampered their versatility. New architectures emerged to address these challenges:

Progressive Growing: This technique trains the GAN on images of increasingly higher resolutions in a step-by-step manner. This allows the model to gradually learn the intricacies of image details, leading to higher-fidelity outputs.

StyleGAN: The Style King Ascends

StyleGAN, a landmark architecture introduced by NVIDIA, stands as a testament to the power of progressive growing and introduces a novel concept: style space. Here's what makes StyleGAN special:

Progressive Growing: StyleGAN leverages the power of progressive growing, allowing it to generate high-resolution images (up to 1024x1024) with exceptional detail and realism.

Style Encoder and Decoder: StyleGAN separates the process of capturing image content from style. An encoder network analyzes an existing image and extracts a latent representation of its style. This style information is then fed into a decoder network, which combines it with random noise to generate a new image that captures the essence of the encoded style.

Style Mixing: StyleGAN allows for mixing styles from different latent codes. This enables fine-grained control over

the generated image's style, allowing for manipulation of factors like color palettes, brushstrokes, or lighting effects.
Beyond StyleGAN: Exploring the Cutting Edge

While StyleGAN has set a high bar, the field of GAN architectures is constantly evolving. Here are some exciting new directions:

Attention Mechanisms: These mechanisms, inspired by transformers, allow the model to focus on specific parts of the latent space during image generation, potentially leading to more control and detail.

Self-Attention GANs (SAGANs): These architectures leverage self-attention mechanisms to allow the model to learn long-range dependencies within the image data, potentially improving image coherence and realism.
The Impact of Advanced Architectures:

The advancements in GAN architectures have led to significant improvements in image generation:

Unprecedented Realism: State-of-the-art GANs can generate images that are indistinguishable from real photographs to the naked eye. This opens doors for applications like creating realistic product prototypes, generating high-fidelity textures for video games, or even manipulating videos in a believable way.

Enhanced Control: Architectures like StyleGAN offer greater control over the style and content of generated images. This empowers artists and designers to explore creative possibilities and produce highly targeted outputs.

Faster Training and Inference: Recent advancements are focused on developing more efficient GAN architectures that require less training time and computational resources. This makes GANs more accessible for deployment in real-world applications.

Looking Forward:

The future of GAN architectures is brimming with potential. As researchers delve deeper into areas like attention mechanisms and explore novel training methodologies, we can expect even more impressive and versatile image generation capabilities. These advancements promise to revolutionize various fields, from art and design to medicine and entertainment.

10.1 Deepfakes and High-Fidelity Image Generation

The ability to generate incredibly realistic images and videos using Generative Adversarial Networks (GANs) has opened doors to exciting possibilities. However, this same technology presents a significant challenge: the creation of deepfakes. Here, we explore the fascinating world of high-fidelity image generation while acknowledging the potential dangers of deepfakes and the need for responsible use.

The Power of High-Fidelity Image Generation:

Unleashing Creativity: GANs empower artists and designers to explore uncharted creative territories. They can generate unique artwork, experiment with different styles, or create realistic textures for video games and animation.

Revolutionizing Design: High-fidelity image generation can be harnessed for product design, allowing for the creation of realistic prototypes or visualizations of new products before physical production begins.

Augmenting Reality: Realistic 3D objects and environments generated by GANs can enhance Augmented Reality experiences, making them more immersive and interactive.

The Dark Side: Deepfakes and their Malicious Potential:

Weaponizing Misinformation: Deepfakes can be used to create fake videos of people saying or doing things they never did. This can be used to damage reputations, sow discord, or manipulate public opinion.

Cybercrime: Deepfakes can be used for identity theft or financial fraud. For example, a deepfake could be used to impersonate someone in a video call to gain access to sensitive information or financial accounts.

Erosion of Trust: The widespread use of deepfakes can erode trust in media and public figures. People may become unsure of what is real and what is fake, hindering healthy discourse and social cohesion.

Combating the Threat:

Deepfake Detection Techniques: Researchers are developing algorithms and tools that can help detect deepfakes with greater accuracy. These tools rely on analyzing subtle inconsistencies in facial movements, lighting, or other visual cues.

Promoting Media Literacy: Educating the public about deepfakes and how to identify them is crucial. People need to be critical consumers of information and not blindly trust everything they see online.

Regulation and Ethical Guidelines: Discussions are ongoing regarding regulations and ethical guidelines for the development and use of deepfake technology. These measures aim to prevent malicious use while fostering responsible innovation.

The Road Ahead:

The ability to generate high-fidelity images and videos is a powerful tool with immense potential. However, it is essential to acknowledge the risks associated with deepfakes and take steps to mitigate them. By promoting responsible development, fostering media literacy, and developing deepfake detection tools, we can harness the power of GANs for good while minimizing the potential for harm.

Here are some additional points to consider:

The line between creative expression and malicious use of deepfakes can be blurry. Striking a balance between freedom of expression and protecting individuals from harm is a complex challenge.

Technological advancements in deepfakes are likely to continue at a rapid pace. Staying ahead of the curve in deepfake detection will be crucial.

The future of high-fidelity image generation lies in responsible development and deployment. By working together, researchers, policymakers, and the public can ensure that this powerful technology is used for positive purposes.

10.2 Ethical Considerations of Advanced GANs

As Generative Adversarial Networks (GANs) evolve, their ability to create high-fidelity images and manipulate reality presents a fascinating paradox. On one hand, they hold immense potential for creativity, innovation, and scientific advancement. On the other hand, their misuse can have detrimental societal consequences. Here, we delve into the ethical considerations that must be addressed alongside the technological advancements of GANs.

The Ethical Minefield:

Weaponizing Misinformation: Deepfakes, a product of advanced GANs, can be used to create fake videos of people saying or doing things they never did. This can be weaponized to spread misinformation, damage reputations, and manipulate public opinion – posing a threat to democracy and social stability.

Privacy Concerns: GANs trained on vast amounts of personal data raise privacy concerns. Techniques like anonymization or differential privacy are crucial to protect individual privacy while enabling the development of this technology.

Bias Amplification: GANs trained on biased data can perpetuate and amplify existing societal biases. This can lead to discriminatory outputs that reinforce stereotypes or disadvantage certain groups.

Job Displacement: As GANs become more sophisticated, they have the potential to automate tasks currently performed by humans, particularly in creative fields like graphic design or photo editing. This raises concerns about job displacement and the need for retraining programs.

The Erosion of Trust: The widespread use of deepfakes can erode trust in media and public figures, making it difficult to distinguish between reality and manipulation. This can hinder healthy discourse and social cohesion.

Navigating the Ethical Landscape:

Transparency and Explainability: Developing more transparent and explainable GAN models is crucial. This allows us to understand how the model generates outputs and identify potential biases.

Data Governance and Fairness: Implementing robust data governance practices and promoting data fairness are essential. This ensures that GANs are trained on unbiased data sets and mitigates the risk of biased outputs.

Regulation and Ethical Guidelines: Developing clear regulations and ethical guidelines for GAN development and deployment is crucial. These guidelines should address issues like data privacy, deepfakes, and potential misuse of the technology.

User Education and Media Literacy: Educating the public about GANs and deepfakes empowers them to become critical consumers of information. People need to be equipped with the skills to assess the authenticity of information encountered online.

Multi-stakeholder Collaboration: Addressing the ethical challenges of GANs requires collaboration between researchers, policymakers, developers, and the public. Open dialogue and a shared responsibility are essential for responsible innovation.

The Path Forward:

Advanced GANs offer a powerful tool with immense potential, but ethical considerations must be paramount. By fostering transparency, promoting data fairness, and creating a framework for responsible development, we can harness the power of GANs for good while mitigating the potential for harm. The future of this technology hinges on our ability to navigate the ethical landscape with foresight and responsibility.

Additional Considerations:

The definition of "harm" and "misuse" can be subjective and context-dependent. Developing a nuanced understanding of these concepts is crucial for ethical decision-making.

The rapid pace of technological advancement necessitates ongoing discussions and adaptation of ethical frameworks to address emerging challenges.

By approaching advanced GANs with a spirit of responsibility and collaboration, we can ensure that this technology serves humanity and paves the way for a brighter future.

www.ingramcontent.com/pod-product-compliance
Lightning Source LLC
LaVergne TN
LVHW051655050326
832903LV00032B/3825